D171703Z

Cover illustration: Preparing and loading 25mm ammunition in an M2 Bradley. The two coloured flags indicate the safety status of the vehicle to the range officers. (S. Zaloga)

1. An M48A5 shepherds a platoon of M113A1s of the 3rd Brigade, California National Guard, at Camp Roberts in 1983. The M113, M113A1 and M113A2 are virtually identical, the main changes being internal improvements. (M. Green)

TANKS ILLUSTRATED NO. 13

US Infantry Combat Vehicles Today

STEVEN J. ZALOGA & MICHAEL GREEN

ARMS AND ARMOUR PRESS

London—Melbourne—Harrisburg, Pa.—Cape Town

Introduction

Tanks Illustrated 13: US Infantry Combat Vehicles Today

Published in 1984 by Arms and Armour Press, Lionel Leventhal Limited, 2–6 Hampstead High Street, London NW3 1QQ; 11 Munro Street, Port Melbourne 3207, Australia; Sanso Centre, 8 Adderley Street, P.O. Box 94, Cape Town 8000, South Africa; Cameron and Kelker Streets, P.O. Box 1831, Harrisburg, Pennsylvania 17105, USA

British Library Cataloguing in Publication Data:
Zaloga, Steven J.
US infantry combat vehicles today. – (Tanks illustrated; 13)
1. Armoured vehicles, Military – United States – Pictorial works
I. Title   II. Series
623.74′75′0973   UG446.5
ISBN 8-85368-663-7

Editing and layout by Roger Chesneau.
Typeset by CCC, printed and bound in Great Britain by William Clowes Limited, Beccles and London.

◀2
2. As with the M901, the main advantage of the hammerhead mount on the M981 is that it enables the vehicle to take up a position with the bulk of the lightly armoured hull hidden from hostile view; here, an M981 FIST shows this tactic. There are currently 970 FIST vehicles entering US Army service. (Emerson Electric)

The companion of the tank on the modern battlefield is the armoured infantry transporter. In the 1950s the US Army adopted the M75, and later the M59, armoured personnel carriers (APCs) for this role. They were not entirely successful, owing to their high cost and to various technical problems, and they were succeeded in the 1960s by the M113 family of vehicles. The M113 series has been the most successful American armoured vehicle since the Second World War: more than 70,000 were built, and they equip over fifty armies around the world. The M113 is typical of the 'battlefield taxis' employed by most armies during the 1960s. It is designed to carry an infantry squad safely to the battle-line, at which point the troops dismount and fight on foot as infantry have done for centuries. In the mid-1960s, however, with the advent of the Soviet BMP-1 and Marder infantry fighting vehicles, armoured infantry transporters began to change: unlike the lightly armed M113s, each now carried a large weapon capable of defeating light armoured vehicles or even tanks; moreover, each was configured to allow its infantry squad to fight from a mounted position.

The United States had already adopted mounted infantry tactics in Vietnam, most notably with the M113 ACAV. However, it was not until the introduction of the M2 Bradley Infantry Fighting Vehicle (IFV) in the early 1980s that the US Army caught up with its European counterparts in this respect. IFVs such as the Bradley are about eight times more expensive than earlier APCs like the M113. The rationale for this is simple: the organization of modern Soviet infantry formations demands a better armed and more mobile vehicle. In the 1950s, when the M113 was designed, Soviet motor rifle divisions had few armoured transporters and only 74 tanks and armoured assault guns. Today, a Soviet motor rifle division has 220 tanks and 579 other armoured vehicles, and, clearly, the .50-calibre gun of the M113 is inadequate against this sort of force. Nevertheless, the M113 will continue to soldier on for decades to come in many roles other than that of an APC, as the M2 gradually takes its place as the primary armoured infantry vehicle.

This book is intended to be a pictorial survey of the many types and variants of armoured infantry vehicles in service with US forces today. Besides the Army types such as the M2 and M113, Marine vehicles like the LVT-7 and LAV series are also depicted. Special emphasis has been given to showing these vehicles from the perspective of their crews, with interior views of many of the versions shown for the first time. Owing to the large number of M113 versions in service, the authors decided against providing coverage of the M113 in Vietnam, as this is given in detail in *Tanks Illustrated 6: Tank War Vietnam*.

In the preparation of this book, help has been provided by many enthusiasts as well as by representatives of the armed services. The authors would like to thank Pierre Touzin, Lieutenant-Colonel James Loop (USA Ret), Brian Gibbs and George Woodard for permission to use their photographs; Colonel Bill Highlander of US Army Public Affairs; Major Bob Reuter, BFV West Coast Field Office; Jim Allingham, Aberdeen Proving Grounds Public Affairs; and Huck Hagenbuch, Max Snavely, Jim Casey and Scott Gourley of the FMC Corporation. Special thanks also go to Major Geishauser, Major Albro and Lieutenant Coletti of the Public Affairs office at Fort Hood for their patient and generous help while the authors were photographing units of the 2nd Armored Division. Finally, a tip of the hat goes to the troops of the 41st Mechanized Infantry (2nd AD) and of the 3rd Brigade, California National Guard, for their good natured support.

Steven Zaloga and Michael Green, 1984

▲3

▲4

◀5

3. The US Army's first fully tracked armoured transporter was the M39 Utility Vehicle, which entered service in 1945. It was not widely used as an infantry transporter because of the unsuitability of its open configuration and the difficulty of debussing in safety. This latter shortcoming is all too evident in this view of a scout squad from the Recce Battalion, I US Corps, dismounting in South Korea, 15 October 1953. (US Army)

4. The first modern US APC was the M44, developed immediately after the Second World War to replace the M3 halftrack infantry transporter. It could carry 27 troops, but it was massive and clumsy and few were built. This prototype is being moved on a T8 Transporter. (US Army)

5. The first APC to be produced in quantity was the M75, which entered service in 1952 and saw limited use in Korea. It was based on light tank components and carried 12 troops. This M75 is seen taking part with the 4th Armored Division in the 'Sage Brush' exercise in Louisiana in November 1955. (US Army)

6. The US Army's first full-scale experience with the new APCs came during the summer exercises of 1953 in Europe. Here, M75s of the 43rd Infantry Battalion support M47 tanks of the 67th Tank Battalion during Exercise 'Monte Carlo' in Germany, September 1953. (US Army)

7. An M75 of the 2nd Armored Division is supported by an M47 tank during Exercise 'Monte Carlo'. The M75 was not amphibious, a drawback which led to the development of the M59, which had that capability (and was less expensive). (US Army)

8. The M59 was amphibious without preparation, which made it more relevant to European terrain criss-crossed with rivers and canals. Here, an M59A1 emerges from Lake Clunie, Alabama, in June 1960 during exercises with the 536th Transportation Company. (US Army)

6▲

7▲

8▶

9. The initial batch of M59s had an externally mounted machine gun but in 1956 the M59A1 was fielded with the machine gun in an M13 cupola, as is evident on this M59A1 of Troop B 3rd Reconnaissance Squadron, 8th Cavalry, 8th Infantry Division, near Kirchen-Bolinden Germany, in October 1958. (US Army)

10. A winter camouflaged M59A1 of the 2nd Brigade, 60th Infantry Division, taking part in the 1962 winter exercise 'Great Bear' in Alaska. (US Army)

11. The M59 could carry a squad of 11 men plus the vehicle commander and driver. One of its main advantages was the easy access provided by this spacious rear door. (US Army)

12. The M59 was plagued with engine problems, and in 1959 the US Army decided to accept the improved M113 in its place. The M113 is very similar in appearance to the M59, although it will be noted that the M113 commander's central hatch is located further back. Here, the squad of an M113 APC of Company C, 31st BG, 7th Infantry Division, form a skirmish line in front of their vehicle in Korea, December 1961. (US Army)

▲9 ▼10

11▲   12▼

9

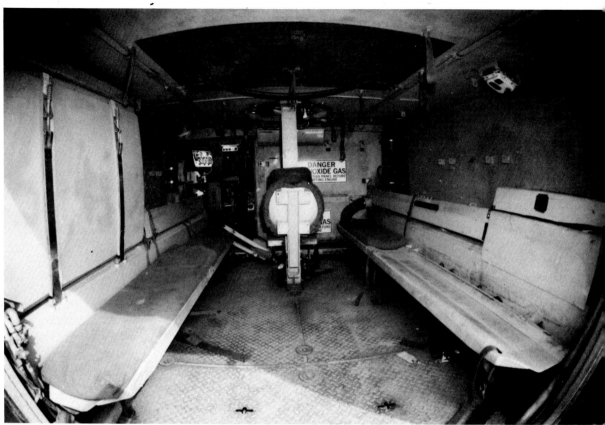

▲13 ▼14

3. The simple layout of the M113A1's interior. The driver's compartment can be seen at the front, far left; in the centre is the squad commander's folding seat which enables him to peer through the top hatch. Behind the bench seats on the left is the fuel tank, kit being stowed on the right. The general finish was originally gloss white, but pale interior green is the current scheme. (S. Zaloga)

4. The M113 has much better amphibious performance than the earlier M59. Here, an M113 crosses a river at Fort Jackson, South Carolina, in June 1966. Water is being drained from the vehicle by a bilge pump and can be seen discharging through a port near the driver. In the water, the M113 is propelled by its tracks. (US Army)

5. In contrast to the almost pristine M113A1 interior shown earlier, this photograph illustrates a well-used M113A1 in the field. A 'standard' piece of equipment in most US APCs is a Coleman cooler for beer, as is very evident on the right-hand bench. On the floor is a .50-calibre ammunition box, some unopened C rations and other stowage. (Brian Gibbs)

6. Besides squad carriers, M113s are frequently configured as command vehicles with additional radios, as is this vehicle of the 2/160th Mechanized Infantry, 40th Infantry Division (Mech), California National Guard, on exercise at Camp Roberts in the summer of 1983. (M. Green)

15▲ 16▼

▲17 ▼18

17. The typical radio layout of a Vietnam-era M113. The radio, mounted immediately behind the driver so as to be accessible to the commander, is an AN/VRC-47 unit consisting of an RT-524A transceiver (upper left), an R-442A 2-channel receiver (upper right) and an intercom unit attached underneath. (US Army)

18. An M113A2 crew takes a breather in the desert scrubland of the US National Training Center in California. This M113 is fitted with the MILES laser simulator equipment, evident in the form of the detector strip along the hull side and the display light on the bow roof. The M2 heavy machine gun is fitted with a blank shredder to permit the use of wood-core training bullets. (M. Green)

19. Probably the least well known armoured transporter in US service is the Soviet MT-LB! Several dozen of these are used by OPFOR units at the National Training Center to simulate Soviet tactics. (M. Green)

20. This M113A1 is finished in a MERDC desert camouflage of sand and field drab with small swathes of sand yellow and black 'crow's feet'; most vehicles of the California National Guard carry this scheme. (M. Green)

21. M113s are also used as ambulances, with litter racks fitted in the rear compartment. Each tank battalion evacuation section has three M113 ambulances, this vehicle being photographed at the 'Reforger' exercise in Germany in September 1982. (Pierre Touzin)

22. Although not as fast as the M2 IFV in cross-country travel, the M113A2 can manage a respectable 40mph on the road, as is evident in the case of this vehicle of the 1/184th Infantry, 40th Infantry Division (Mech). There are some 9,300 M113s in the US Army today, making it the most widely used US armoured vehicle; about 3,500 serve with National Guard units like this one. (M. Green)

23. Even though the M2 IFV is beginning to replace the M113 in mechanized infantry battalions, some M113s remain as command vehicles. This M113A2 of the 41st Infantry – the first unit to convert to the M2, in 1983 at Fort Hood, Texas – is an example. (S. Zaloga)

▲21

▲22 ▼23

24▲ 25▼

26▼

24. An M113A1 passes an M88A1 Medium Recovery Vehicle of the 149th Armored Division at Camp Roberts in the summer of 1983. (M. Green)

25. Radio equipment commonly installed in current M113s is this AN/VRC-64. It consists of a transceiver (left) and an intercom (right), and is a variation of the common PRC-77 radio adapted to vehicles. Incidentally, the interior finish of this vehicle, an M106 mortar carrier, is overall forest green. (S. Zaloga)

26. An M113A2 of the 2nd Armored Division equipped with additional radios for its role as a command vehicle. It lacks the large bow splash plate which is used when the vehicle is swimming. This particular M113 was in service in the 1980 'Reforger' exercise in Germany. (Pierre Touzin)

▲27

◄28

27. Experience in Vietnam led to the development of Armoured Cavalry Assault Vehicle (ACAV) kits to protect the main hull gunner and two rear M60 gunners; the kit is shown in place on an M113 of the 11th Armored Cavalry at Fort Meade in July 1966 before the unit was shipped to Vietnam. The kit is not in current use on US Army M113s. (US Army)

28. Details of the M60 machine gun mount as used in the M113 ACAV. (US Army)

29. The large roof hatch of the M113 is popular with its crews since the interior of the vehicle is uncomfortable during long road marches, although the US Army still discourages the use of M113s for mounted combat against heavily defended positions. (M. Green)

30. One little known piece of equipment carried by M113s of scout sections of armoured cavalry platoons is the viscous damped mount permitting the firing of the M47 Dragon anti-tank missile; on this vehicle, the shield for the mount can be seen to the left of the M2 heavy machine gun. The large band on the side of this M113A2 of the 1st Armored Division is a velcro strap for attaching a MILES training device detector band, whilst the circular orange insignia bearing the number '36' is a temporary manoeuvre marking used by the Orange Army during the 'Reforger' exercises held in Germany every September. (Pierre Touzin)

29 ▶

30 ▼

1. Another example of the Dragon mount on a M113 of the 1st Armored Division. The missile tube protrudes through the circular port in the left of the shield when loaded. (Pierre Touzin)

2. The M577 command post is the second most common version of the M113 series after the basic APC, some 2,900 being currently in service with the US Army. This M577A1 carries the name 'The Elite Ones' on the bowplate. Additional fuel and water is carried on the roof, together with a portable generator to power lights and the vehicle's many radios. This M577 took part in the 1978 'Reforger' exercises. (Pierre Touzin)

3. The interior of the M577A1, left-hand side. The large map table is folded down, and above this is a shelf for the many radios carried by these command vehicles. The higher sides of the M577 were designed to allow unit commanders to stand up while examining maps. (Brian Gibbs)

4. The right-hand side of the M577A1 interior. The triangular devices on the wall map are azimuth calculators in green covers. With the map tables folded down the bench seats below can be folded out in their place. (Brian Gibbs)

5. A key item in the equipment of an M577 this auxiliary power unit which provides electricity for the vehicle's many radios and lights when the engine is turned off. (Brian Gibbs)

33▲

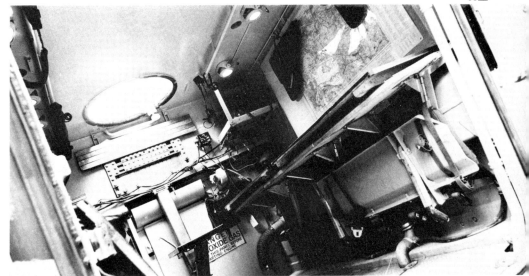

34▲ 35▼

▲36 ▼37

38.▲

39.▲ 40.▼

36. The stowage on the rear of an M577 consists of a large tent that can be extended off the vehicle to provide command staff with more space when the vehicle is stationary. (Brian Gibbs)

37. An M577A1 of the 3/67th Armored, an M1 tank battalion of the 2nd Armored Division, at Fort Hood in 1983. The M577 is the standard command vehicle in all US Army mechanized units, be they tank, infantry, cavalry or artillery. (S. Zaloga)

38. One of the lesser known M113 variants is the XM233E1 TOW Missile Carrier, which consists of an M220 TOW anti-tank missile mount on an M113A1 chassis. Although fairly common, with some 1,400 in service, it so closely resembles the standard M113 that it is seldom noticed: when not in use, the M220 mount telescopes into the hull, making the vehicle virtually indistinguishable from the M113. This XM233E1/M113 was in use with the 61st Infantry, 5th Infantry Division, at Fort Polk, Louisiana, in August 1977.

39. A close-up view of an extended M220 TOW mount on an XM233E1 TOW Missile Carrier. (FMC)

40. An interior view of an XM233E1 TOW carrier with the M220 mount folded down inside the vehicle. The racks to the right are used to carry ten additional TOW rounds; the square platform in the foreground is folded up to provide a base for the two-man TOW crew; and the stowage box forward is used to carry TOW gear. (Brian Gibbs)

▲41 ▼42

41. An M113/TOW vehicle of the 3rd Infantry alongside a Canadian Leopard tank during the 1977 'Reforger' exercises. This vehicle is fitted with a TOW-CAP kevlar fabric armour shield over the TOW launcher, an expedient adopted prior to the introduction of the fully protected M901 ITV (Improved TOW Vehicle). Twelve of these equip mechanized infantry battalions, for anti-tank protection. (US Army)

42. A more satisfactory solution to the need for a tank destroyer version of the M113, the new M901 ITV mounts two TOW missile launchers on an elevating trunnion which enables the ITV to hide behind a hill. In this fashion, the M901 does not have to expose its thin armour to the wrath of enemy tank fire. (Emerson Electric)

43. A close-up photograph of the launcher on the M901 ITV. The large opening in the centre is for the launcher sights, and the launcher is reloaded by tilting it backwards towards the rear hatch. (Emerson Electric)

44. Not surprisingly, the M901 ITV is commonly called 'The Hammerhead' by its troops. There are currently over 1,000 of these vehicles in service, mainly with support companies. The conversion is carried out by Emerson Electric, the basic chassis coming from the FMC Corporation. (Emerson Electric)

44▼

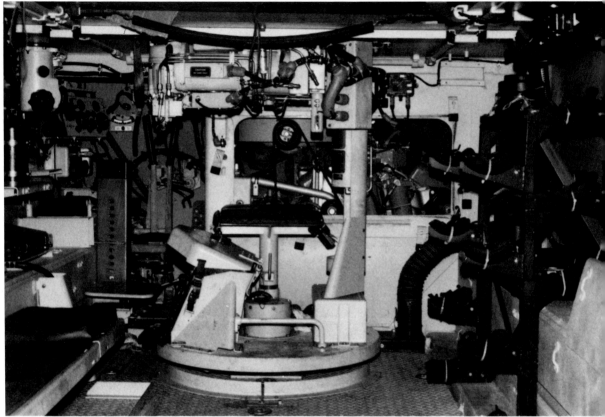

▲45

▲46

45. A view showing the interior of the M901 ITV. The gunner sits in the circular turret mount, with the loader stationed on the bench to the left and the additional TOW rounds to the right. (George Woodard)

46. An M901 ITV of the 4th Infantry Division (Mech). During transit, the hammerhead mounting is folded down and locked on the rear deck to prevent damage. (Pierre Touzin)

47. An M113 command vehicle attached to a battalion of M2 Bradley IFVs of the 41st Infantry, 2nd Armored Division, Fort Hood, Texas, July 1983. (S. Zaloga)

48. An M113A1 in the desert wastes of the National Training Center in California. (M. Green)

47▲   48▼

49. Troops of the 193rd Infantry dismount from the M2 IFV. The M2 first entered service in 1983, and will gradually replace M113 infantry transporters in divisions equipped with the M1 Abrams tank. (Hughes)

▲50　▼51

50. An M113 finished in the new three-colour camouflage scheme adopted by the US Army in 1984. (US Army)
51. M2 Bradleys at Fort Hood, July 1983.
52. The M981 FIST (Fire Support Team vehicle), used by artillery forward observers, is almost identical with the M901 ITV, being distinguishable principally by its greater number of radio antennae. In lieu of the TOW missile launch tubes, the hammerhead mount contains electro-optical sensors and a laser designator (V/GLLD) which can be used to guide semi-active, anti-tank projectiles like the M712 Copperhead, or Hellfire anti-tank missiles, precisely to their targets. (Emerson Electric)

52▼

53. This M901 clearly shows the travelling configuration of the hammerhead mount. Also evident are the large velcro bands for the MILES simulator detector strips on the hull sides. (Pierre Touzin)

54. The M125 is a mortar carrier version of the M113, armed with an 81mm weapon; currently, 794 of these vehicles serve with the US Army. The mortar is mounted on a fully traversing pedestal and fires through split circular hatches in the vehicle's roof. (FMC)

55. An M125 81mm mortar carrier of the 40th National Guard Infantry Division prepares to fire on the ranges at Camp Roberts in 1983. (M. Green)

56. A front three-quarter view of a factory-fresh M125 mortar carrier. The baseplates for firing the mortars away from the carrier are stowed on the hull side, a feature which distinguishes mortar carriers from ordinary APCs. (FMC)

▲53 ▼54

55▲   56▼

▲57

57. A rear view of the M106 mortar carrier. Externally the M106 is essentially similar to the M125 but carries the heavier 4.2in mortar on a revised firing platform. There are 1,140 M106s in US Army service, of which 487 equip the National Guard. They are used by mechanized infantry and tank units to provide fire support, illumination and smoke coverage. (FMC)

58. An M106 mortar chief sights his 4.2in mortar before firing. (M. Green)

59. In contrast to the square roof hatches on the M113, the M106 and M125 have larger, circular, split hatches, as is evident here. (S. Zaloga)

60. A close-up of the 4.2in mortar mount in an M106 mortar carrier. The interiors of these carriers are painted forest green or in olive drab camouflage rather than the usual interior green colour since the vehicles often operate with their hatches open. (S. Zaloga)

61. A view of the left-hand side stowage racks in the M106 carrier. This vehicle is fully stowed except for ammunition. (S. Zaloga)

62. The right-hand ammunition stowage racks in the M106 carrier. Some water jerrycans have been left in the racks where the ammunition is usually stored. (S. Zaloga)

58▲ 59▼

60▼

61▼

62▼

▲63 ▼64

65▲

3. An M106 4.2in mortar carrier photographed during the 1983 'Reforger' exercises in Germany as a member of the 'Blue Army'. (Pierre Touzin)
4. The M163 Vulcan Air Defense System (VADS) mates an M741 carrier with a 6-barrelled Vulcan automatic cannon for the air defence of mechanized columns; the M163A1 is fitted with a range-only radar. This vehicle took part in the 1978 'Reforger' exercises. (Pierre Touzin)
5. A pair of M163A1s cross an Armored Vehicle Launched Bridge (AVLB) positioned by the M60 AVLB transporter in the background during the 1973 'Reforger' exercises in Germany. There are at the moment over 300 M163A1s in service with the US Army, but after they have been modernized under the PIVADS programme they will be transferred to the National Guard as Regular Army units receive the new M247 Sergeant York DIVAD gun system. (US Army)
66. An interior view showing the main turret assembly of the M163 VADS. (S. Zaloga)

66▼

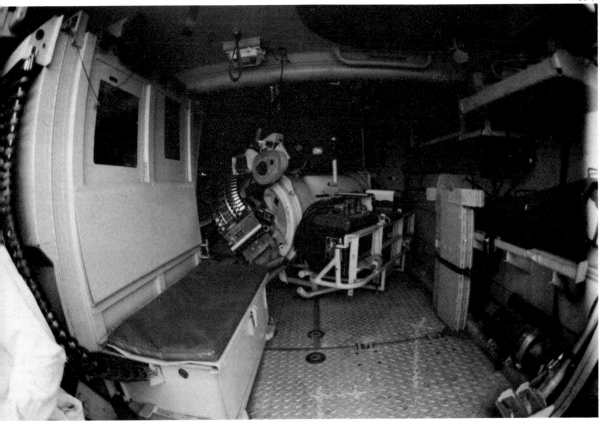

▲67

▲68

67. A close-up of the turret of an M163A1 VADS, the radar antenna visible in the upper right corner of the photograph. The large white oval object to the left is a protective helmet used during proving grounds trials. (S. Zaloga)

68. A close-up of the right-hand side of the M163A1 turret. There is some distortion of the image owing to the use of a very wide angle lens. (S. Zaloga)

69. The M48 Chaparral air defence system consists of a ground-launched derivative of the Sidewinder air-to-air-missile fired from an M730 tracked vehicle; the M730 is in turn a derivative of the M113/M548 design. There are 520 of these units in US Army use, for low-altitude air defence of mechanized columns. This

particular vehicle, which does not have the missiles fitted to the rear racks, serves with 2nd Armored Division at Fort Hood, Texas. (S. Zaloga)

70. The M752 Lance is a tactical battlefield missile, either conventional- or nuclear-tipped (but designed primarily for the latter). It is the short-range counterpart to the Pershing missile and is launched from a chassis derived from the M113. (Pierre Touzin)

71. The M548, an unarmoured transporter based on the M113 chassis, is used mainly for carrying supplies for mechanized units, notably for self-propelled howitzer batteries. There are about 1,400 examples in service with the US Army. (M. Green)

▼69

70▲ 71▼

37

▲72 ▼73

72. The M548 is also used to carry electronic shelters, as is the M101⁵ Teampack (shown), which is a combination of the M548 with an Emerson Electric AN/MSQ-103A Teampack Radar Monitoring System mounted in the rear bed. (Emerson Electric)

73. In the mid-1960s, the Infantry School at Fort Benning modified an M113 with exterior firing ports in an effort to permit the crew to fight from within the vehicle. This experiment led to the improved XM765. (US Army)

74. Although the XM765 was not accepted for US service use (owing to interest in a more powerfully engined version), it was sold to Belgium, the Netherlands and the Philippines. The illustration shows a Dutch YM765 PRAT tank destroyer, which uses the same TOW hammerhead mounting as the M901 ITV. (Emerson)

75. The XM765 led to the XM723 MICV of the early 1970s, which offered better armour protection and a larger engine. This rear view of the XM723 shows how much gear an infantry combat vehicle carries in battle. (FMC)

74▲ 75▼

76. In the mid 1970s, the Army combined the requirement for its new infantry carrier with that for a new cavalry scout vehicle. The cavalry insisted on a two-man turret and a TOW missile launcher to provide more firepower, and this led to the development of the XM723 into the M2 Infantry Fighting Vehicle and the M3 Cavalry Fighting Vehicle, collectively known as the Bradley Fighting Vehicle System (BFV). This photograph shows the main 25mm turret armament of the BFV in action. (Hughes)

77. The twin-tube TOW missile launcher on an M2 IFV in the raised, firing position. The dismounted squad is equipped with an M249 SAW, M60 LMG, Dragon anti-tank missile, M249 SAW and an M16A1 rifle. In the vehicle, each member of the crew has an additional M231 Firing Port Weapon (FPW), a derivative of the M16A1 which fires only on automatic. (Hughes)

78. An M2 of the 41st Infantry/2nd Armored Division (the first fully operational M2 Bradley unit) at Fort Hood in 1983. (S. Zaloga)

79. An M2 during loading. The Bradley is fitted with an M242 25mm chain gun in the turret plus an M240 7.62mm coaxial machine gun, ammunition for both weapons being stowed in the rear troop compartment as well as in the turret. The boxes above the smoke mortars carry extra smoke grenades, and the other external racks carry additional 7.62mm ammunition. (S. Zaloga)

80. Troops prepare their weapons before embarking on tactical live-fire exercises. Individual weapons are loaded, and the 25mm Bushmaster ammunition is loaded into links with a mixture of anti-armour, high-explosive and incendiary projectiles depending on the mission. (S. Zaloga)

78▲

79▲ 80▼

▲81

81. The crews of two Bradleys take a breather while their infantry squads prepare. There are two permanent crew members in the Bradleys, the driver and the gunner, the second seat in the turret being occupied by the squad commander, who dismounts in action. (S. Zaloga)

82. The sleeker sides of the BFV mean that it cannot swim unprepared like the M113. Instead, a flexible screen is stored within the hull sides which is erected to give the vehicle enough freeboard to float. The upper portion of the screen can be seen projecting here. (S. Zaloga)

▼82

83. Crews finish mounting into the Bradley before setting off on their mission. The M2 to the left is loaded with TOW missiles, as is evident by the removal of the canvas protective cover from the rear of the launch rack. (S. Zaloga)

84. The Bradley is fairly cramped inside, and so a good deal of personal stowage is carried elsewhere: for example, tarps and other gear are often lashed down to the front of the vehicle, as shown in this photograph. (S. Zaloga)

▲85

85. A platoon of M2s moves out. The current mechanized infantry platoon consists of four M2s, a platoon commander and three rifle squads; each squad consists of nine men, the two M2 crewmen and seven troops. Although smaller, the modern squad carries considerably more firepower than its older counterpart. (S. Zaloga)

86. A rifle squad moves out. The FPWs have not yet been fitted to the gun ports, nor have the rubberized covers over the swimming screens been tucked in, so showing the location of these features along the upper edges of the hull sides. (S. Zaloga)

87. An M2 Bradley IFV prepares to move out for live-fire exercises at Fort Hood. (S. Zaloga)

88. One of the new LVTP-7A1 amtraks at Camp Pendelton, California, in 1984. The vehicle carries the standard four-colour MERDC camouflage. (M. Green)

▼86

89. Although this M2 appears to be painted a sand colour, in fact it has just returned from desert tests at the Yuma Proving Ground where it became caked with dust. The raised skirts provide a glimpse of usually concealed suspension details. (US Army)

▲90 ▼91

0. One of the first operational Marine LAVs, in this case an LAV Recovery Vehicle, at Camp Pendelton in February 1984. (M. Green)
1. This view of the LAV-Logistics vehicle shows its raised rear hull. (GM-Canada)
2. An M2 moving across country: the vehicle can manage 35–40mph over terrain like these dry Texas prairies. The turret is fully stabilized, allowing the gun to be aimed accurately even when moving speedily in rough conditions. (S. Zaloga)
93. A dismounted M2 squad in action. No men are readily visible, since most are hiding or crawling through the dry prairie grass, whilst the M2 is partly concealed in a shallow gully. (S. Zaloga)

▲94

▲95 ▼96

94. A TOW missile round is loaded into its two-round launcher. Loading can take place with minimum risk to the loader, thanks to th design of the hatch.

95. A TOW round is fired, the TOW itself evident to the extreme left of the photograph. The target was on a hillock some 2km away and was a direct hit. The TOW and Improved TOW (I-TOW) can defeat any known Soviet tank and thus give the M2 and M3 considerable firepower against armour. Although the Bushmaster gun canno destroy a tank frontally it can penetrate side armour at close ranges more importantly, it can easily penetrate the armour of Soviet infantry combat vehicles at very long ranges. (S. Zaloga)

96. A pair of M2s in 'retrograde' manoeuvres. Platoons usually fall back with one or two vehicles in static overwatch positions to provide covering fire, while the other two vehicles withdraw. In this case, the two overwatch vehicles are out of sigh (S. Zaloga)

97. Small numbers of M2 Bradleys began to be delivered to the US 7th Army in Europe in 1983, and this example was one of the first operational vehicles. (M. Green)

98. A Bradley has its turret installed. The turret, with its full stabilization, thermal night sights, guns and other sophisticated features, accounts for over 60 per cent of the cost of the vehicle. (M. Green)

97▲   98▼

▲99 ▼100

▼101

99. The Bradley passed its extensive Army developmental tests with flying colours, and indeed exceeded the requirements in many categories. This was in no small measure due to the experience of the FMC Corporation design teams who had been responsible for the earlier M113 and LVT-7 series. (US Army)

100. The business end of the Bradley: a view into the turret of the BFV. The gunner sits to the left and the commander to the right. The commander has a supplementary set of controls which allows him to operate the vehicle's weapons if necessary. (S. Zaloga)

101. The gunner's station in a BFV. The hand controls for the gun can be seen below the main sight unit. (S. Zaloga)

102. The crawl space on the left-hand side of the turret leads to the driver's station. The floor in this crawl space would normally be covered with ammunition boxes in a loaded vehicle. (S. Zaloga)

103. The commander's station in the BFV. At the far left is the breech of the M242 Bushmaster 25mm autocannon, and at the extreme right is the vehicular radio. At the top centre of the photograph is the commander's optical elbow sight which affords him the same view as that available to the gunner. (S. Zaloga)

102▲   103▼

▲104

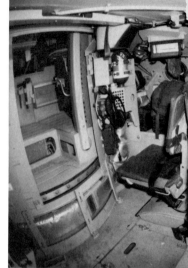

▲107

▲105 ▼106

▲108 ▼109

110▲

111▲

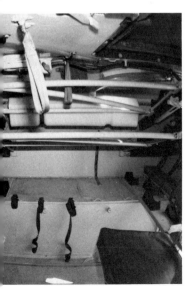

104. Externally, the main difference between the M2 and M3 is the absence of an operable firing port and sighting periscopes on the M3; this view shows the closed firing port and periscope locations of the latter. Future production M3s may have a revised rear roof hatch. (S. Zaloga)

105. The sighting periscope and firing port of an M2 IFV. (S. Zaloga)

106. The rifleman's view from the Bradley is surprisingly good, as is evident from this photograph taken through a Bradley periscope. (S. Zaloga)

107. The right-hand side of the rear troop compartment of the M2. The centre seat is folded up, but otherwise the vehicle is fully stowed and ready for action. (S. Zaloga)

108. The left-hand side of the M2's rear troop compartment. In this case, TOW rounds are stowed, though Dragon rounds can also be carried. The rear section accommodates seven fully equipped riflemen. (S. Zaloga)

109. The right-hand side of the rear compartment of the M3 CFV. Only two scouts are carried in the CFV, so the extra room is used to hold additional ammunition. The racks seen here are used to carry TOW rounds. (S. Zaloga)

110. The rear compartment of the M3 CFV, left-hand side, showing the seats for the two scouts and the extensive space for 25mm ammunition stowage. (S. Zaloga)

111. A fully stowed M3 CFV. The black plastic boxes contain 25mm ammunition and the olive drab tubes hold TOW missiles. (M. Green)

▲112 ▼113

12. An M2 Bradley on trials in Germany in the summer of 1983. As well as being faster and better armed than the M113, the M2/M3 is also considerably better protected with special aluminium/steel laminate armour. (M. Green)

13. The commander of a Bradley has an open ring sight mounted externally on the vehicle which enables him to 'rough aim' the gun when he is outside. In the background is an M163A1 VADS. (S. Zaloga)

14. An M2 of the 41st Infantry engages targets at the firing ranges at Fort Hood. (US Army)

15. Another M2 at the firing ranges at Fort Hood. (US Army)

16. The Marine Corps equivalent of the M113 and M2 is the LVTP-7. Here an M113A2 and an LVTP-7A1 are parked side by side, giving some idea of the considerable difference in size between these two vehicles. (M. Green)

114▲

115▲ 116▼

▲117 ▼118

17. The forerunner of the LVT-7 series was the LVT-5 series which was employed in Vietnam. This is an LVTE-5A1 engineer vehicle, popularly called the 'Potato Digger' by Marines in Vietnam. This particular LVT is seen in operation with the 7th Marines south of Danang in August 1968. The LVT-5 series proved too cumbersome and fire prone, and was replaced by the -7 series in the 1970s. (USMC)

118. LVTP-7s charge ashore at Camp Pendelton, California, during tactical exercises. These massive amphibians carry 24 troops, double the capacity of the M113. (M. Green)

119. A rear view of an LVTP-7, showing the traversing nozzles for the water jets that propel these vehicles in the water. It is interesting to note that, automotively, the Bradley series is derived from the LVT-7 series rather than from the M113 owing to the need for more durable components. (FMC)

120. A view of the cavernous interior of an LVTP-7. The bench seats of the vehicle are folded away, adding to the impression of size. (FMC)

119▲ 120▼

▲121

121. Among the variants in the LVT-7 series is the LVTR-7 recovery vehicle, which is used to repair and evacuate damaged LVT-7s. Its large crane is very evident in this view. (USMC)
122. The LVTC-7 is the command version in the series and is fitted with additional radios, as is apparent in this rear view. (FMC)

▼122

123. Another photograph showing the inside of an LVTC-7, looking in from above with the top roof hatches open. (FMC)
124. An LVTP-7 splashes ashore with a beach control party giving instructions. This is the early LVTP-7, witness the circular headlight ports in the bow; on the later LVTP-7A1, these ports are rectangular. (M. Green)

123▲ 124▼

▲125

125. A rear view of an LVTP-7A1. Although this photograph does not show the square front headlight configuration, the other distinctive feature of the version, the slightly raised commander's cupola, can be seen. (M. Green)

126. This front view of an LVTP-7A1 clearly shows the vehicle's distinctive rectangular headlight configuration. There are currently nearly 1,000 LVT-7s of both types in Marine service. (M. Green)

127. A pair of Marine LVTP-7A1s pass over the beach landing area at Camp Pendelton. The LVT-7 has good cross-country performance, but being a rather large and vulnerable target it is not intended for use against defended positions. (M. Green)

128. An LVTP-7 with its water propulsion jets pointed forward to prevent sand ingestion from material thrown up by the tracks. (M. Green)

129. The crew of an LVTP-7 check the engine covers. The LVT series is the only type of armoured vehicle currently in service which can survive and continue to run even though completely submerged for 30 seconds. (M. Green)

▲126 ▼127

128▲ 129▼

▲130 ▼131

132▲

130. A dramatic view of an LVTP-7 re-entering the water to return to ship. (M. Green)

131. An LVT-7 has considerable freeboard and buoyancy in water, especially when empty, as can be seen in this photograph of LVTP-7. (M. Green)

132. A formation of LVTP-7s returns to its mother-ship. (M. Green)

133. LVTs are carried by nearly all US amphibious warfare ships, that in the background here being an LST. Most LVT servicing is carried out on board ship. (M. Green)

133▼

▲134 ▼135

136▲

134. Because of the unsuitability of the LVT-7 series for conducting combat operations far from shore, the Marines have begun to acquire the new LAV. This will serve as their equivalent of the Army's M2/M3 series. It is built by GM-Canada and is based on the Swiss Mowag Piranha design. A prime consideration in its adoption was ease of transport, a requirement quite evidently met, as this photograph of an LAV with its C-141 transporter shows. (GM-Canada)

135. Besides the Marine LAV-25, the Army has attempted to

adopt a similar version for its new light divisions. This LAV-25, with a special TOW missile launcher added, was displayed to Army and Congressional officials in 1983 in the hopes of reviving the programme after Congress had cancelled it the previous year. (S. Zaloga)

136. The LAV-25 is armed with the same 25mm Bushmaster chain gun as the M2/M3 Bradley. This is the prototype of the TOW launcher LAV-25. (S. Zaloga)

▲137　▼138

37. Like the M2, the LAV is designed to permit its troops to
~~ght~~ fight from within the vehicle. This shows the right-hand side of
~~he~~ the interior of the LAV-25 troop carrier. (S. Zaloga)
38. This view of the left-hand side of the LAV-25's troop
~~ompartment~~ compartment also shows the rear of the turret basket, which

houses a two-man crew. (S. Zaloga)
139. The turret interior of the LAV. (S. Zaloga)
140. Lacking the track propulsion of the M113, the LAV uses a
conventional propeller for power in the water. (S. Zaloga)

▲142 ▼143

141. (Previous spread)
The LAV-M mortar
carrier mounts an
81mm weapon that can
be fired from within the
confines of the vehicle
or from a dismounted
position. (S. Zaloga)
142. The LAV-AT
tank destroyer is fitted
with the same Emerson
hammerhead TOW
mount as the Army's
M901 ITV. (GM-
Canada)
143. The LAV-
Logistics vehicle is
designed to carry
supplies for an LAV
assault force, the LAV
itself being intended for
use by small, highly
mobile and self-
sufficient assault groups.
(GM-Canada)